SMALL FRY

Jaime Adoff illustrated by **Mike Reed**

Dutton Children's Books

For Anaya Grace, *my* small fry...
—J. A.

For Jane, Alex, and Joe
—M. R.

DUTTON CHILDREN'S BOOKS
A division of Penguin Young Readers Group

Published by the Penguin Group

Penguin Group (USA) Inc., 375 Hudson Street, New York, New York 10014, U.S.A. • Penguin Group (Canada), 90 Eglinton Avenue East, Suite 700, Toronto, Ontario, Canada M4P 2Y3 (a division of Pearson Penguin Canada Inc.) • Penguin Books Ltd, 80 Strand, London WC2R 0RL, England • Penguin Ireland, 25 St Stephen's Green, Dublin 2, Ireland (a division of Penguin Books Ltd) • Penguin Group (Australia), 250 Camberwell Road, Camberwell, Victoria 3124, Australia (a division of Pearson Australia Group Pty Ltd) • Penguin Books India Pvt Ltd, 11 Community Centre, Panchsheel Park, New Delhi—110 017, India • Penguin Group (NZ), 67 Apollo Drive, Rosedale, North Shore 0632, New Zealand (a division of Pearson New Zealand Ltd) • Penguin Books (South Africa) (Pty) Ltd, 24 Sturdee Avenue, Rosebank, Johannesburg 2196, South Africa • Penguin Books Ltd, Registered Offices: 80 Strand, London WC2R 0RL, England

Text copyright © 2008 by Jaime Adoff
Illustrations copyright © 2008 by Mike Reed
All rights reserved.

CIP Data is available.

Published in the United States by Dutton Children's Books,
a division of Penguin Young Readers Group
345 Hudson Street, New York, New York 10014
www.penguin.com/youngreaders

Designed by Jason Henry
Manufactured in China • First Edition
ISBN: 978-0-525-46935-3

1 3 5 7 9 10 8 6 4 2

SMALL FRY

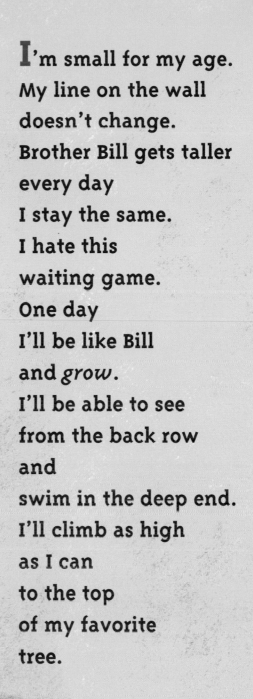

I'm small for my age.
My line on the wall
doesn't change.
Brother Bill gets taller
every day
I stay the same.
I hate this
waiting game.
One day
I'll be like Bill
and *grow*.
I'll be able to see
from the back row
and
swim in the deep end.
I'll climb as high
as I can
to the top
of my favorite
tree.

My name
won't always be

Small fry.

MOVIE

Big head in front,
left, right, big head on every side.
Dad brings encyclopedia
A through G, props me up so I can see.
High above these big head trees.
Now I have the very best seat.
The lights go out.
Time to eat!
I dive into my
BiG bag of
Chocolate Gobs,
take a sip of my Soda pop.
Now I'm ready to watch the
Movie.

Big Sis

getting ready
for
1st date.
I watch
make
up
Lip
stick
Neck
lace
Ear
ring
Brace
let...
Big Sis.

Big
and
Small er
fast and
slow er

We grow
different
speeds
We grow
different ways
We grow
up
together.

Pass it to me, one bounce
I freeze.
Legs out of gas
shoes are flat.
Under the hoop I shoot.
Nothin' but backboard.
I'm still too short.
BENCH!
Warms my rear end
Tomorrow, my REVENGE...

My ball has no basket
before it,
just DODGE.
I'm "Air Shortness."
My four foot frame
built just for *this* game.
The Ball blasts towards me
a billion times light speed.

I DODGE the
　　BALL
like it wasn't there at all.
I can duck under, jump over, swerve around,
do my math problems, feet never touch the ground
while I Dodge the Ball.
Everyone knows my name, in every hall
all over school.
I'm Dodge Ball

"Air Shortness" to you....

"AIR SHORTNESS"

Witches

Cackling in the curtains.
I wake up in a cold sweat.
Want to run fast to my parents' bed.
If I was bigger I could fight.
Knock that witch out
into the cold cold night.
But Mom says,
"Two wrongs don't
make a right."
So I'll sit tight.
I know
The three
words witches hate.
Learned them in school, yesterday.

I hope it works, guess I'll try.
I stand tall
Raise my hands high.
Open my mouth
can't believe what comes out.
"I'M
NOT
AFRAID!!!"

Wait,
what was that?
Cackling?

I'll be right back....

VERY BIG MARK

rolls up on me
wants my lunch money
or
ELSE!
I give him a few bills,
Monopoly cash.
Let's see him spend that.
Very Big Mark's gonna be
a little short at lunch.

Dear Principal Davis:

Ricky has to go home for

Lunch and he won't be

back until tomorrow.

I think he's getting a fever.

Ricky's Mother

MoM AND DaD

Tell me what to do.
"**GO TO BED.**"
"**GO TO SCHOOL.**"
"**CLEAN YOUR ROOM.**"
"Why do I have to?"
"**BECAUSE WE SAY SO.**"
"Why do you get to say so?"
"**BECAUSE WE'RE MOM AND DAD.**"
OK.
Just thought I'd ask.

NO FUN ALLOWED!

"You have to be this ☞ - - - - - - - - tall to ride me."

It's times like these
I wish I couldn't read.

WHEN AM I GONNA GROW?

Is there a magic
cookie?
I hope so.
I'll eat it
right before bed,
in the morning
I'll be taller than
Dad.
Looking
Down
I'll be a grown Up.
No more short stuff.
Won't have to go
to school again.
Just play with my
friends...

Dad says I'd miss
everything,
new clothes
Growing Pains.
(*OUCH!*)
Dad says,
"Step by step
wait your turn
growing up is how you
learn."
He might be right
but first, I'll take a bite
of that magic cookie.

COOL FUN
FORT FOREVER . . .

Me, Max,
and my dog, Pepper.
No one can find us there
not even Mom and Dad.
We bring candy, cookies, and
potato chips.
Max stands while
me and Pepper sit.
Our spaceship blasts high,
the S.S. Small Fry.
We stop on planet OR-E-O.
Have a few cookies, then it's time to go.
Pepper barks when it's almost dark.

We land just in time for supper.

PARENT-TEACHER CONFERENCE

Underneath my chair
hands over ears,
eyes shut tight,

I'm invisible.

TiM

is my best friend.
Doesn't matter, that I'm
bigger than him.
We do everything together.
Play and pretend,
we're Police and Firemen.
Tim has the best video games too.
We play every day, after school.
  At the park, Tim speeds fast
down the slide.
  We hide and go seek,
until Mom calls, "Time to eat."

Watching TV...

we whisper about
what we're gonna be
when we
get
older....

Ice-Cream Truck

I hear the song
from 2 blocks.
Me and Jack
run fast
we're just in time...
but there's a line
ten kids deep.
I slither my way
between legs,
backward slide—
twisting and turning
I'm an ice-cream spy.

Before anyone knows
I'm in the front row.
I get two fudgy bar blasts
pass one back to Jack.
In the blink of an eye
We're out of sight........
(2 minutes and 37 seconds later.....)

On my front steps,
  me and Jack
slurp our fudgy bar blasts.
We don't say a word—

just laugh,
and laugh,
and
laugh.

RECESS

Always picked last.
I say I can catch,
they see
smallest kid in class.
"Okay, I'll take Jake."
Todd makes a face.
But today is the day.
First play
I go
L O N G
I scream,
"TODD THROW ME THE BALL."

He tries to look away,
Todd says, *"Shoo fly you're botherin' me."*
I know time's on my side
'cause
here come the big guys
could eat Todd in just one bite.
He looks left, right, shakes his head
everyone is covered but me.
I'm sooooo open, I'm in the next town.
"THROW ME THE BALL!"

Todd's almost down
but the ball
is on its way
on its way
today is the day.
First play
I go
L O N G

Todd Throws *Me* the ball...
I told them I could catch.

Recess
always picked ~~last~~ first.

In The Crowd

I get scared.
People rushing,
pushing, shoving past,
Mom and Dad
and me.
I can barely see the
sign flash
"Walk."
I feel lost.

Then a huge crush
of elbows and arms
squeeze me
closer to Mom.
Dad lifts me up over
the

CROWD

looks like an ocean.

People waves—crash
into street corner shores.
Splashing over blocks into
buildings and stores.

We sail across
and dock—
at The FunToy Shop.

In *this* crowd
I *know* my way around.

SMALL SOLDIER

I am the only one for the job.
There is no one else.
I am a soldier going into battle.
My unit waits outside the field.
I crawl on hands and knees,
dark surrounds me.
I'm ready for anything.
There is no sound, I feel and touch
my way around,
breathing through my mouth.
"Almost...
almost in my hands..."
"Got it!" I shout.

My mission, almost impossible, is complete.
I got the Wiffle ball from Bongo's doghouse.
This poem will self-destruct in ten seconds.
9
8
7
6
5
4 (I'd turn the page if I was you)
3
2 (last chance........)
1

WHACK!

The ball *flies* off my bat
I'm almost to third
in seconds flat.
SAFE!
Brush myself off.
I cut this diamond up.
THREE FOR THREE today.

Pitchers cringe when I come their way.
They call me "little hurt."
I make baseballs cry.
Go all the way home on a pop fly.
Now that's fast.
In the field, I wheel and deal
turn a double play on my knees.

In the stands everyone screams:
GO!   BOB!   EEEEE !   GO!

There are no small ballplayers.
Just small bats.

Whack.

SLEEP OVER

Inside my souped up
sleeping bag
I laugh so hard
I almost cry.
Steve makes
a face like he's
the nose in
*Attack of the
nine hundred and
twelve foot sneeze.*

I can almost see it
blowing up Cleveland.
Ha Cheeeeeeew!
Colonel Kleenex
to the rescue!
We all fall on the floor.
Lean over and listen
to Tommy snore.

I cover his mouth,
"Stop it!" he shouts.
We stay up late
talk about girls and ghosts
and what we like most
about school,
(LUNCH!)

Inside our souped up
sleeping bags
we laugh so hard
we almost cry.
All night
long....

I wear an S on my chest
Super Small Fry
Able to leap big
bullies in a single bound.
I can crawl on the ground
under their radar.
Use my power
to get all A's in class.

I can run fast
slip inside
a small space
and hide.
NEVER!
I stand and fight
for the little guy.
Super Small Fry
always saves the day!